P9-DME-826

HELLO! ☺

THIS POSITIVITY KIT BELONGS TO:

The Positivity Kit

LISA CURRIE

A TarcherPerigee Book

An imprint of Penguin Random House LLC
375 Hudson Street
New York, New York 10014

First trade paperback edition 2016

Copyright © 2016 by Lisa Currie

Penguin supports copyright. Copyright fuels creativity, encourages diverse voices, promotes free speech, and creates a vibrant culture. Thank you for buying an authorized edition of this book and for complying with copyright laws by not reproducing, scanning, or distributing any part of it in any form without permission. You are supporting writers and allowing Penguin to continue to publish books for every reader.

Tarcher and Perigee are registered trademarks, and the colophon is a trademark of Penguin Random House LLC.

Most TarcherPerigee books are available at special quantity discounts for bulk purchase for sales promotions, premiums, fund-raising, and educational needs. Special books or book excerpts also can be created to fit specific needs. For details, write: Special markets @penguinrandomhouse.com

ISBN 9780399175978

Printed in the United States of America

9 10

Book design by Lisa Currie

YOU NEED TO LET
THE *little things* THAT
WOULD ORDINARILY BORE YOU
SUDDENLY *thrill you.*

•ANDY WARHOL•

Please note:

THIS IS *not* A BOOK TO JUST LOOK AT.

IT'S A CREATIVE SPACE FOR YOU TO draw, write, doodle over AND cut & paste.

SOON IT'LL BE A CATALOG OF EVERYTHING THAT MAKES YOU FEEL good AND excited.

SOON IT'LL BE A HANDMADE MAP THAT CAN GUIDE YOU BACK TO YOUR HAPPIEST SELF, BACK TO YOUR sweet spot IN LIFE.

WHENEVER YOU NEED IT.

let's begin!

WRITE YOURSELF A MESSAGE IN THE SKY!
SOMETHING THAT WOULD MAKE YOU SMILE
IF YOU SAW IT.

nice little moments
BOTTLED UP!

THE BLISSFUL SILENCE WHEN

THE WAY MY BODY FEELS AFTER

6

THE SWEET ANTICIPATION OF

GETTING HOME TO FIND

colors
that make
me happy

AN ACTUAL DREAM COME TRUE!

9

* FILL THIS PAGE WITH ALL THE GOOD THINGS YOU'VE DONE IN YOUR LIFE SO FAR. BIG THINGS & LITTLE THINGS. THINK OF AS MANY AS YOU CAN!

DONE!

A CUTE CONVERSATION I HAD WITH A STRANGER

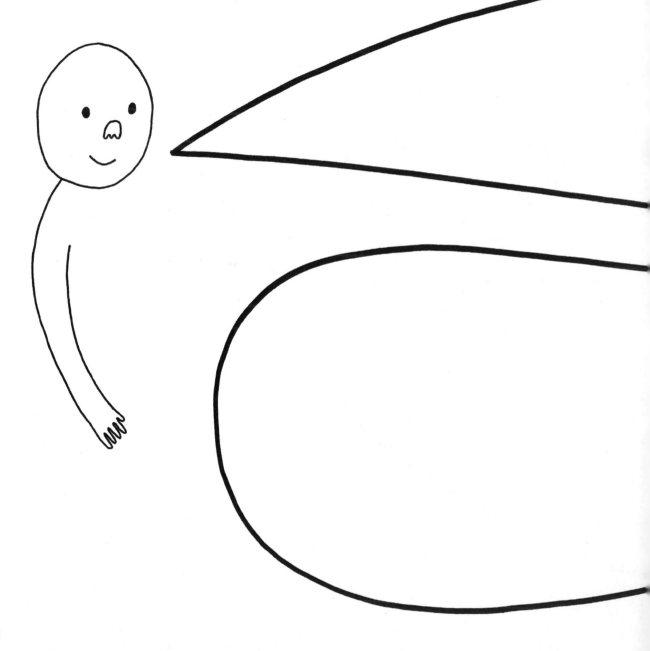

☐ IN REAL LIFE   ☐ IN MY DAYDREAMS

13

Catalog of good things

A

A My all-time favorite condiment.

B This sweet compliment someone once gave me.

C This invention, because it's the best!

D This nice moment in my daily routine.

E Giggling with my friends about...

F When the kitchen smells like...

G This photo I found on the internet.

B

15

THE ULTIMATE HAPPY SONG MASHUP!

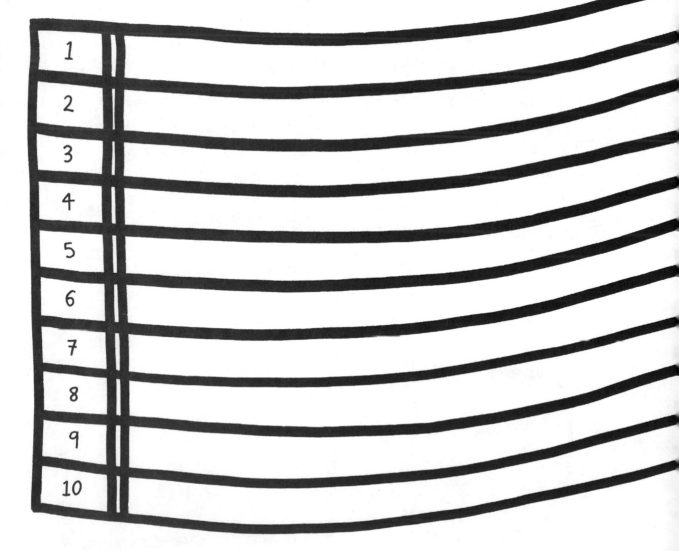

WHAT ARE THE <u>TEN</u> HAPPIEST SONGS YOU LOVE?
WRITE DOWN ONE LYRIC FROM EACH SONG TO
CREATE THE ULTIMATE MASHUP!

MIXED BY

DJ _____
(what's your DJ name?)

CONGRATULATIONS to me!

I GOT THAT THING THAT I ALWAYS WANTED!

a smell that reminds
me of someone
I love very much:

FEELING THANKFUL

I'VE GOT SOMEONE IN MY LIFE WHO KNOWS
HOW TO _____
_____

I'VE GOT SOMEONE IN MY LIFE I CAN TALK TO
ABOUT _____
_____

I'VE GOT SOMEONE IN MY LIFE WHO MAKES
THE BEST EVER _____
_____

I'VE GOT SOMEONE IN MY LIFE WHO I CAN
CALL WHEN _____
_____

I'VE GOT SOMEONE IN MY LIFE WHO _____
_____

SOUVENIRS FROM THE
ADVENTURES
I'VE BEEN ON!

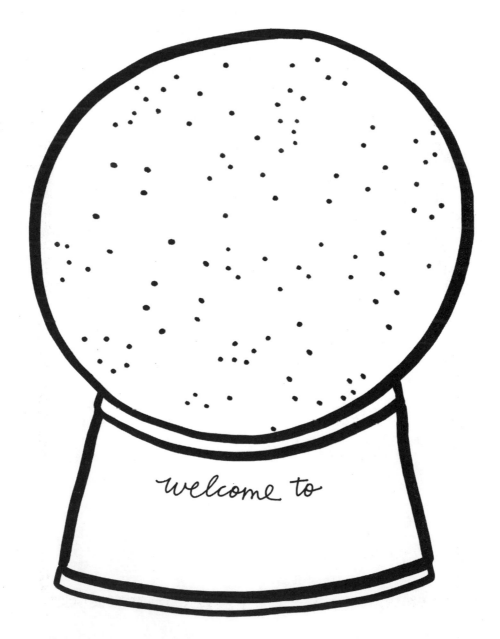

welcome to

I WENT TO

AND ALL I GOT WAS
THIS awesome
T-SHIRT!

all the places I hope

to visit one day ✈

BEST FRIEND APPRECIATION PAGE

MY BEST FRIEND'S NAME:

NICKNAME:

EMOJIS THAT BEST DESCRIBE HIM/HER:

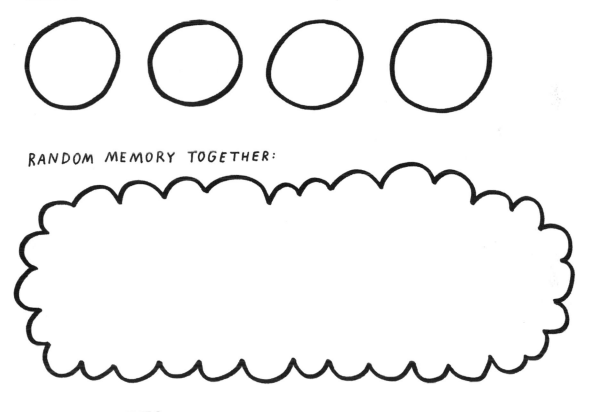

RANDOM MEMORY TOGETHER:

THE SOUNDTRACK TO OUR FRIENDSHIP:

IF WE WERE IN A BAND TOGETHER IT'D BE CALLED:

HOW MUCH I LOVE MY BESTIE:

(MEH) (A LITTLE BIT) (SO MUCH) (THE MOST!)

ATTENTION: SEVEN NEW HOLIDAYS

ARE BEING INTRODUCED THIS WEEK!

(MAKE SURE YOU CELEBRATE THEM)

monday is...

DAY!

tuesday is...

DAY!

wednesday is...

DAY!

thursday is...

DAY!

friday is...

DAY!

saturday is...

DAY!

sunday is...

DAY!

RECENT MOMENTS

OF PURE JOY

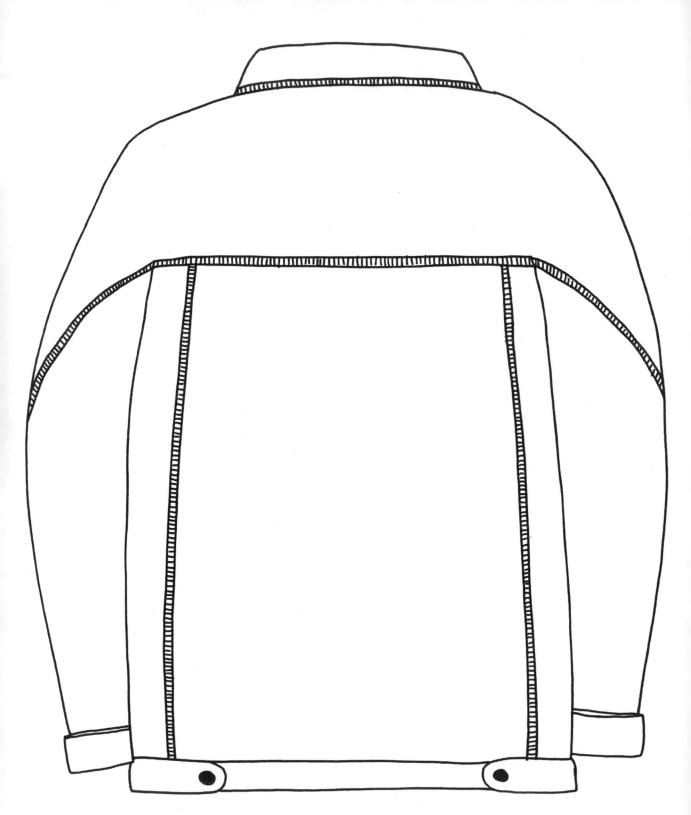

Positivity Jacket

THAT WAS FUN!

THANKFUL FOR TODAY

yes!

love is all you need

FRIENDS FOR ALWAYS

← CUT & PASTE THESE PATCHES ONTO YOUR JACKET
OR MAKE SOME OF YOUR OWN!

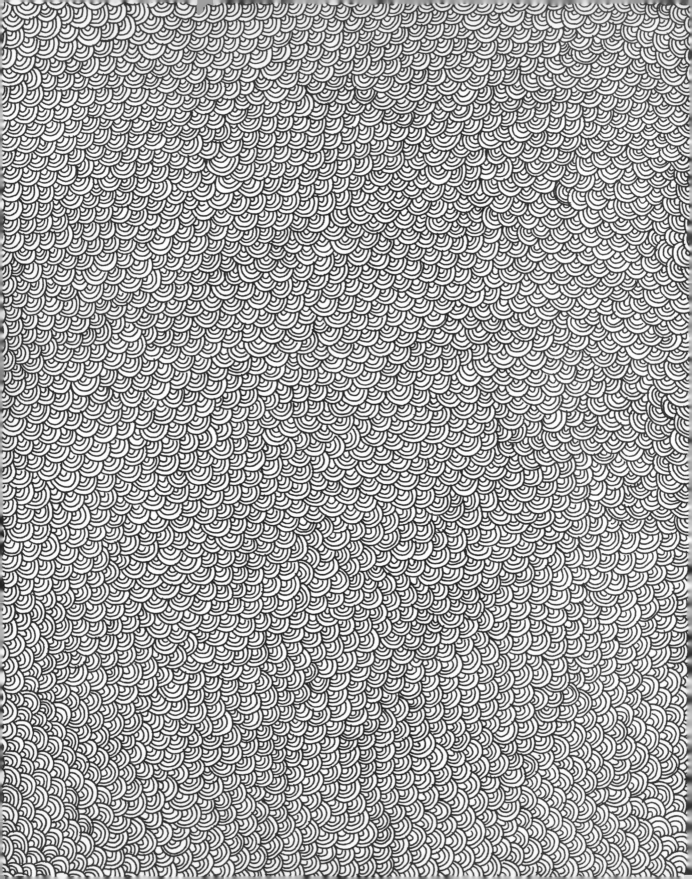

BRAVERY AWARD

FOR: _____

(your name here)

Because even though you were
nervous to _____

_____

_____ you did it anyway.

A NAMING CEREMONY FOR THE LITTLE THINGS THAT ARE IMPORTANT TO ME

MY PHONE!

I SHALL NAME YOU:

BECAUSE:

MY TOOTHBRUSH!

I SHALL NAME YOU:

BECAUSE:

MY FAVORITE MUG!

I SHALL NAME YOU:

BECAUSE:

MY LUCKY
UNDERWEAR!

I SHALL NAME YOU:

BECAUSE:

wish list

got list

DID YOU EVER KNOW
THAT YOU'RE MY HERO?

MY HERO IS:

BECAUSE:

THREE WAYS THEY'RE SIMILAR TO ME:

1 - WE'RE BOTH _____

_____

2 - WE'RE BOTH _____

_____

3 - WE'RE BOTH _____

_____

MY FAVORITE THING I'VE HEARD THEM SAY:

CREATE A SOUNDTRACK FOR THIS BOOK &
INCLUDE ALL YOUR FAVORITE FEEL-GOOD SONGS!

1 _____

2 _____

3 _____

4 _____

5 _____

6 _____

7 _____

8 _____

9 _____

10 _____

ESCAPE to PARADISE!

YOU'VE JUST ARRIVED AT "POSITIVITY ISLAND" FOR A WEEK-LONG GETAWAY!

who did you bring with you?

what essentials did you pack in your luggage?

THIS ALBUM
TO ENJOY
ON REPEAT:

THIS OUTFIT TO
RELAX IN:

THIS BOOK
TO GET
LOST IN:

Oh — and there's a chef
on the island. What
will you ask him to
cook for you?

FUN WORDS TO SAY ALOUD

snickerdoodle!

haberdashery!

46

MONDAY

TUESDAY

Design yourself
a novelty mug
for every day
of the week!

WEDNESDAY

THURSDAY

48

FRIDAY

SATURDAY

Something to make you
smile as you sip your
morning coffee/tea!

SUNDAY

49

GOOD CHOICES I'VE MADE IN MY LIFE SO FAR

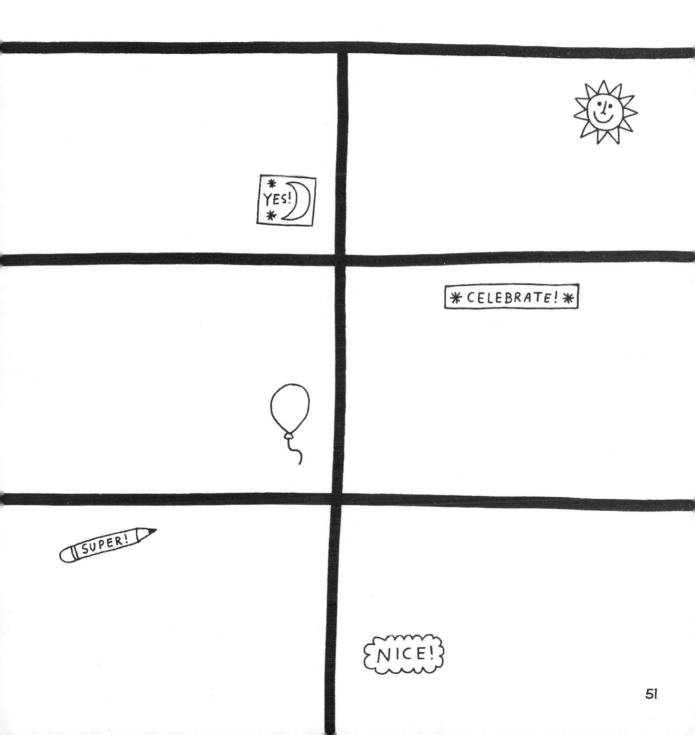

51

♡ LETTER TO MY 👀

TO MY DEAREST EYEBALLS,

I HOPE YOU KNOW HOW SPECIAL YOU ARE TO ME.

WITHOUT YOU I COULDN'T MAKE EYE CONTACT WITH
A CUTE STRANGER ON THE TRAIN , OR MAKE
EYE CONTACT WITH MY CUTE SELF IN THE MIRROR!

WITHOUT YOU I COULDN'T _____
_____

OR SEE WHAT _____ LOOKS LIKE.

MY CLEVER EYEBALLS, YOU MAKE IT POSSIBLE TO
_____
_____
_____ AND _____
_____

HOW COULD I EVEN _____
_____ WITHOUT YOU?

OH, MAN. WE'VE SEEN SUCH AMAZING THINGS
TOGETHER, LIKE _____

_____

_____ , REMEMBER THAT?

THE LITTLE THINGS, TOO. LIKE A GLIMPSE OF

_____

AND HOW IT ALWAYS MAKES ME SMILE.

EVEN WRITING THIS LOVE LETTER. I COULDN'T
SEE THE PAGE WITHOUT YOU GUYS.

I LOVE YOU BOTH!

OR SHOULD I SAY, 👁 LOVE YOU BOTH! HA-HA.

    XOXO _____

PS. THIS IS A PORTRAIT I DREW OF YOU GUYS:

HAPPY PANTS!

DESIGNED by YOU!

☺ FABRIC SO SOFT IT FEELS LIKE _____

_____

☺ A SECRET POCKET FILLED WITH _____

_____

☺ NO MATTER HOW LONG YOU WEAR THEM THEY ALWAYS SMELL LIKE _____

☺ OTHER FEATURES WORTH MENTIONING:

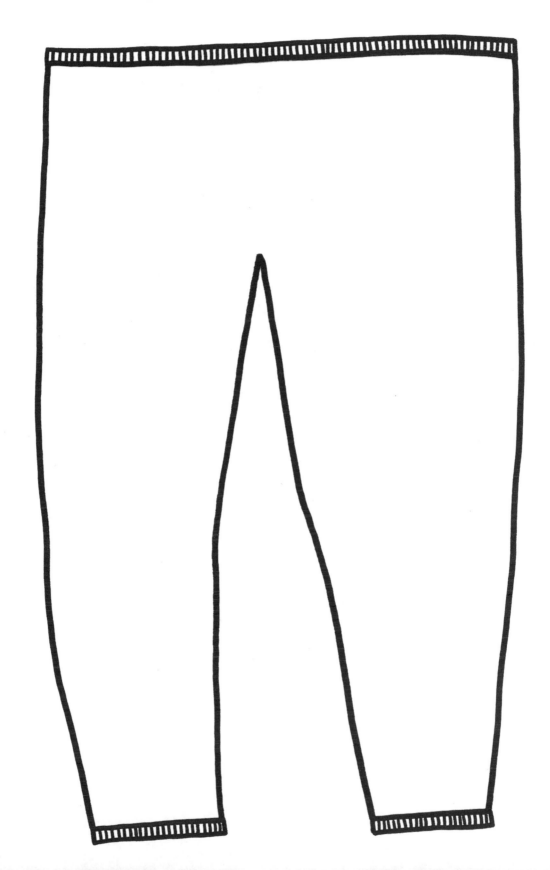

A BEAUTIFUL SUNRISE

WHERE I WAS:

WHO I WAS WITH:

WHAT I WAS WEARING:

WHAT WAS ON MY MIND:

A PERFECT SUNSET

WHERE I WAS:

WHO I WAS WITH:

WHAT I WAS WEARING:

WHAT WAS ON MY MIND:

SMALL *but* SATISFYING VICTORIES I'VE HAD RECENTLY

① DRAW A PORTRAIT OF SOMEONE WHO'S HELPED YOU RECENTLY — IN A BIG OR SMALL WAY.

② NOW WRITE THAT PERSON A LETTER OF GRATITUDE. EXPLAIN HOW MUCH THEIR HELP REALLY MEANT TO YOU ⟶

THANK YOU!

TO:

FROM:

PS:

(3) GIVE THEM THE LETTER IF YOU CAN! ♡

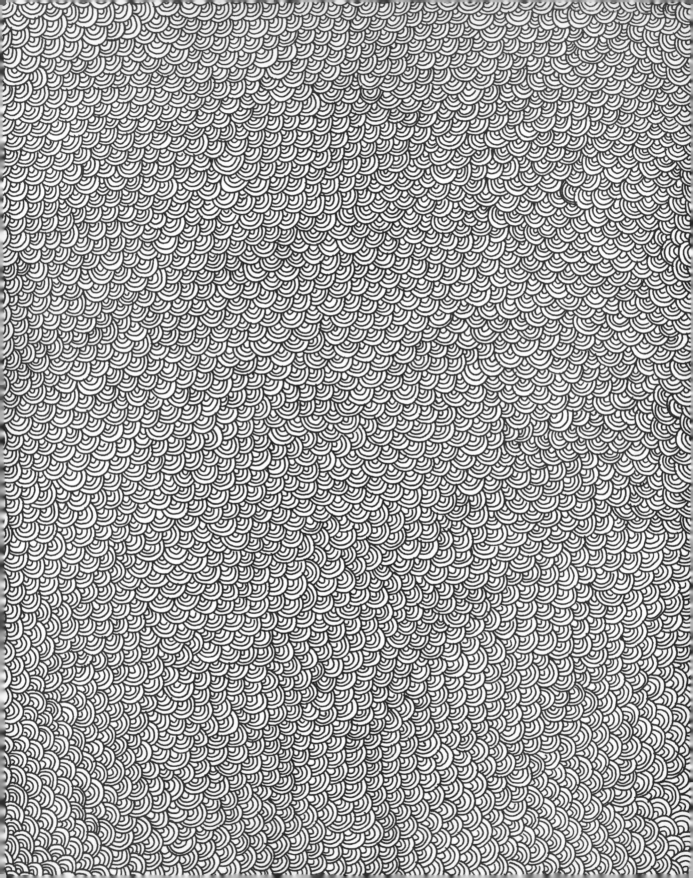

THE *best* THINGS in LIFE ARE FREE!

FOR EXAMPLE:

	$0.00
	$0.00
	$0.00
	$0.00
	$0.00
	$0.00
	$0.00
	$0.00
	$0.00
	$0.00

③ QUICK WAYS TO MAKE ME LAUGH!

① SEND ME A HILARIOUS PHOTO LIKE THIS ONE

② WATCH THIS FUNNY VIDEO WITH ME

③ REMIND ME OF THIS MOMENT THAT MADE ME
LAUGH SO HARD I (ALMOST) PEED MY PANTS

best DANCE MOVES
I'VE EVER TRIED

* THE SASSY TORNADO
← SELF-HUG SPAGHETTI LEGS
* "ALL THE SINGLE LADIES"
*
*
*
*
*
*
*
*

(MAKE UP SOME OF YOUR OWN!)

IMPORTANT SOUNDS IN MY LIFE...

THE SOUND I LOVE FALLING ASLEEP TO:

MY FAVORITE SOUND TO WAKE UP TO:

THE SOUND I MISS FROM MY CHILDHOOD:

THE SOUND THAT ALWAYS MAKES ME LAUGH:

THE SOUND THAT MAKES ME FEEL SAFE:

▶

THE SOUND THAT MAKES ME FEEL EXCITED:

▶

WHAT "HOME" SOUNDS LIKE TO ME:

▶

THE SOUND THAT REMINDS ME OF BEING ON HOLIDAY:

▶

THE SOUND THAT REMINDS ME OF SOMEONE I LOVE:

▶

MAP OF MY
HAPPY PLACES

Dear _____,

Roses are red
Violets are blue
I like your _____
and your _____, too!

Bananas are yellow
Honey is sweet
You're a total _____
From your head to your feet!

Dolphins are clever
I have two knees
I'm asking you nicely
Will you _____, please?

Love from _____ ♡ ♡

PS: _____

WHAT MY DREAM HOME LOOKS LIKE

ESSENTIAL ITEMS
(check all that apply)

☐ lots of house plants
☐ indoor waterfall
☐ lickable wallpaper
☐ ocean views
☐ city views
☐ secret reading nook
☐ indoor mini golf
☐ popcorn machine
☐ sunflower garden
☐ emergency taco delivery chute
☐ painting of a dolphin

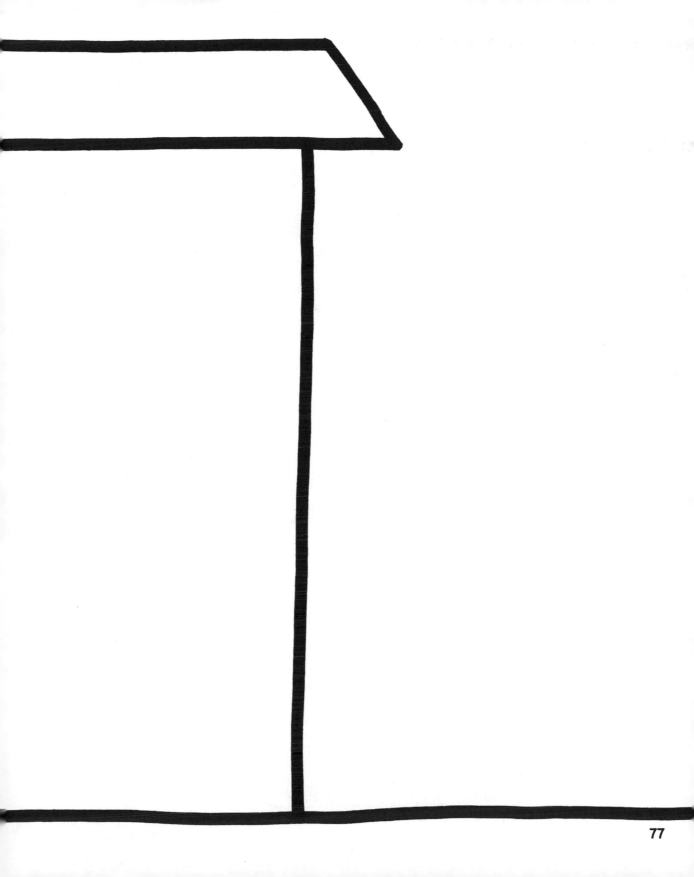

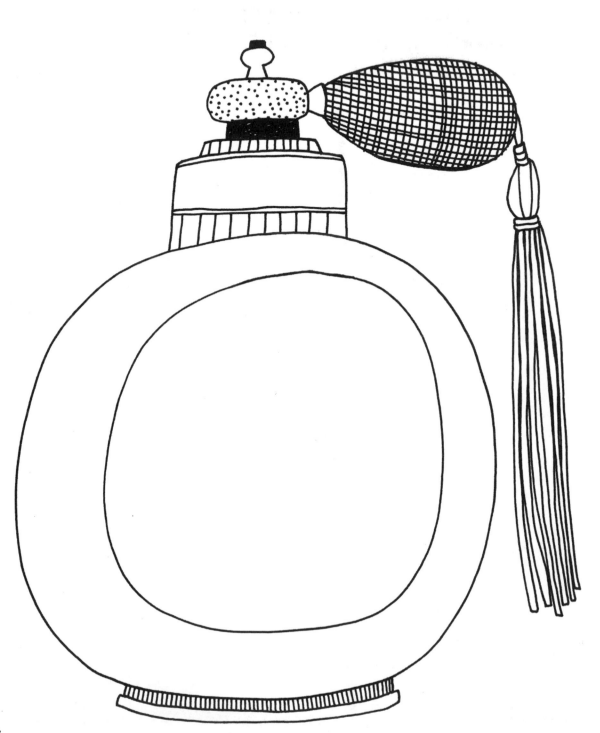

FIVE OF THE BEST
smells

① THE UNMISTAKABLE, TOTALLY DELIGHTFUL
SCENT OF _____

_____

② THE SWEET SMELL OF _____

_____ IN THE MORNING.

③ A SPECIAL WHIFF OF _____

_____

④ THE COMFORTING SMELL _____
THAT REMINDS ME OF MY _____

_____

⑤ _____

_____

my favorite quotes from

my favorite movies

SUPER HERO
REGISTRATION FORM

YOUR HUMAN NAME: _____

YOUR SUPERHERO NAME: _____

WHAT ARE YOUR SUPERPOWERS?

* SUPER QUICK AT _____

_____

* EXCELLENT MEMORY FOR _____

_____

* AMAZINGLY GOOD AT _____

_____

* _____

_____

WHEN WAS THE LAST TIME YOU FOUGHT CRIME, OR JUST TRIED TO MAKE THE WORLD A LITTLE BETTER? (ONE EXAMPLE WILL DO)

_____

_____

_____

_____

PLEASE SUBMIT A DRAWING/DIAGRAM OF YOUR SUPERHERO OUTFIT & ACCESSORIES:

✱ FORM CAN BE SUBMITTED TO YOUR NEAREST SECRET SUPERHERO LAIR FOR CONSIDERATION.

THESE ARE A FEW of my FAVORITE things...

A IS FOR

B IS FOR

C IS FOR

D IS FOR

 IS FOR

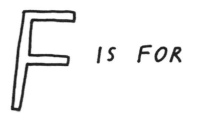 IS FOR

 IS FOR

 IS FOR

I IS FOR

 IS FOR

K IS FOR

L IS FOR

M IS FOR

N IS FOR

 IS FOR

 IS FOR

 IS FOR

 IS FOR

S IS FOR

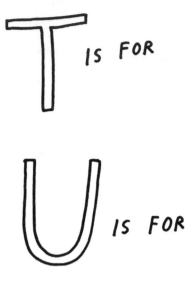 IS FOR

U IS FOR

V IS FOR

W IS FOR

 IS FOR

 IS FOR

Z IS FOR

MEMORIES OF A

Very Yummy Dinner

FIRST UP WAS THE ENTREE!

A LUSCIOUS SERVING OF _____

I HAD ONLY ___ BITES BEFORE THE WHOLE PLATE HAD DISAPPEARED INTO NOTHING BUT A SCRUMPTIOUS MEMORY.

THEN CAME THE MAIN COURSE!

I WAS DELIGHTED TO SEE _____
COOKED TO PERFECTION, SERVED WITH _____
AND A GARNISH OF _____
THE TASTE WAS DELICATE, BUT ALSO ROBUST, AND IT REMINDED ME OF _____ FOR SOME REASON?

LASTLY, THE DESSERT.

IT WAS A SPECIAL TREAT CALLED "_____
_____"

A REFRESHING FUSION OF _____

AND _____. THE SECRET INGREDIENT WAS ACTUALLY _____ IF YOU CAN BELIEVE!

AFTER DINNER ALL I COULD DO WAS GIVE MYSELF A GENTLE BELLY RUB AND _____

the end

my all-time favorite

BAD* PUNS & SILLY JOKES

✳ SO BAD, THEY'RE GOOD!

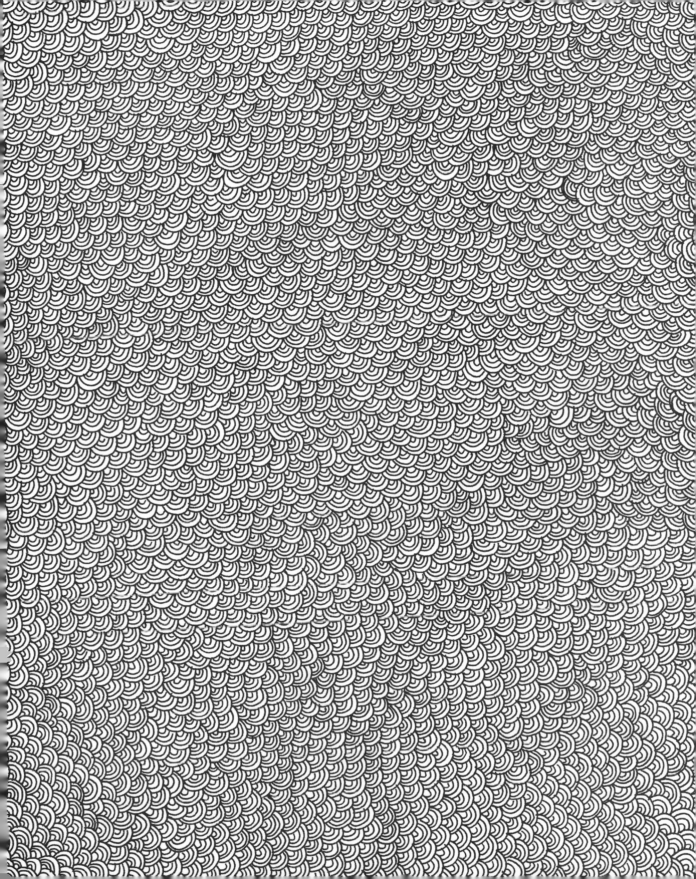

MAKE A MASCOT FOR YOURSELF!
TO HYPE YOU UP BEFORE A BIG DAY
(OR ANY DAY!)

GO GIRL!

GO BOY!

you got this

SHOULDER PADS!

TEAM YOU!

looking GOOD!

* cut and paste these body parts
94 or draw/collage some of your own!

MY MASCOT'S NAME IS _____

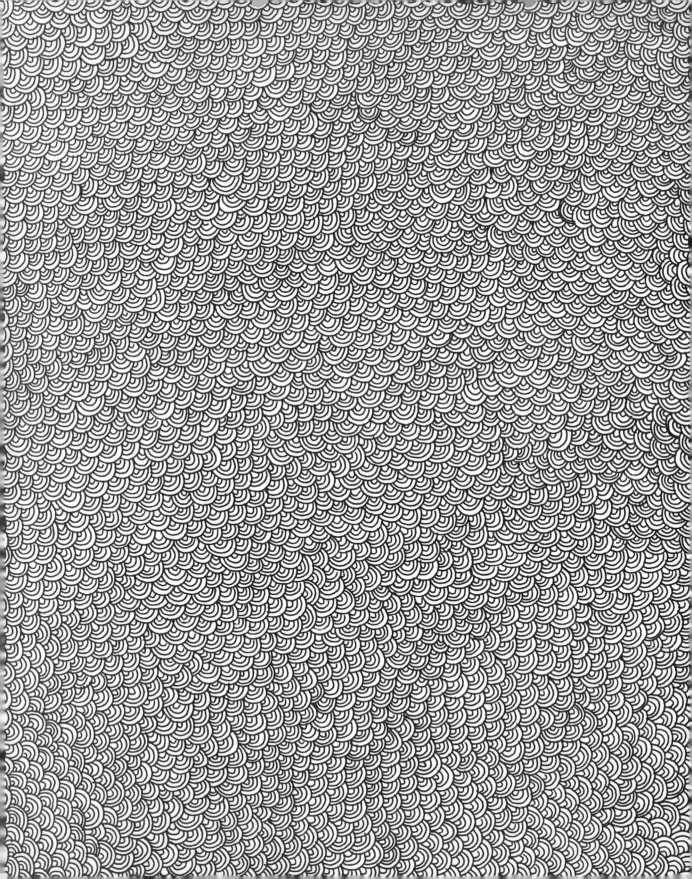

Greetings from my BED!

POPULATION: ME

Hi _____

Just wanted to send you a postcard to say I miss you — but having such an awesome time here!

What have I been up to? Well...

See you soon! x _____

WHAT I'M OBSESSED WITH RIGHT NOW...

make a wish!

twenty

nineteen

eighteen

seventeen

sixteen

fifteen

fourteen

thirteen

twelve

eleven

ten

nine

eight

seven

six

five

four

three

two

one

TOP 20
COUNT
DOWN
best moments of
MY LIFE SO FAR!

✳ DRESS THE MODEL IN YOUR FAVORITE OUTFIT
TO LAZE AROUND THE HOUSE IN.

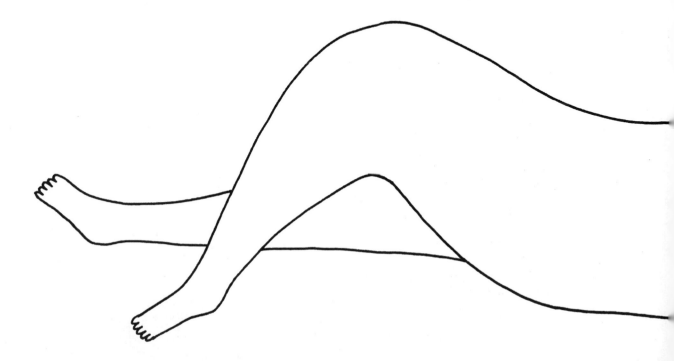

The Greatest Music

11 Am:

12 Pm:

2 Pm:

4 Pm:

6 Pm:

8 Pm:

10 Pm:

12 Am:

Festival Ever! (EVER) (WE'RE SERIOUS)

SPECIAL EVENTS

- In the chill-out space there'll be _____
  filled with _____
  and an unlimited supply of _____

- In the craft tent there'll be a workshop with the
  one-and-only _____
  who'll be teaching us to make _____

- Special acoustic duet by _____
  and _____
  All audience members must wear _____

FOOD TRUCKS

It's a good day when _____

_____

It's a good day when _____

_____

It's a good day when _____

_____

It's a good day when _____

_____

It's a good day when _____

_____

It's a good day when _____

_____

It's a good day when _____

_____

It's a good day when _____

_____

It's a good day when _____

_____

It's a good day when _____

_____

It's a good day when _____

_____

It's a good day when _____

_____

It's a good day when _____

_____

It's a good day when _____

_____

It's a good day when _____

_____

✳ FINISH THIS SENTENCE WITH AS MANY DIFFERENT
ANSWERS AS YOU CAN THINK OF...

THE MUSEUM OF STUFF & THINGS THAT ARE PRECIOUS TO ME

EXHIBIT A:
MY FAVORITE BOOK
PRECIOUS TO ME BECAUSE:

EXHIBIT B:
THIS PIECE OF JEWELRY
PRECIOUS TO ME BECAUSE:

EXHIBIT C:

THIS LETTER/NOTE
PRECIOUS TO ME BECAUSE:

EXHIBIT E:
THIS TINY KEEPSAKE
PRECIOUS TO ME BECAUSE:

EXHIBIT D:
THIS ARTWORK
PRECIOUS TO ME BECAUSE:

who do you hope they're from?

I've always wanted to try this:

BEGINNERS' CLASS!

ALL WELCOME!

WHEN:

WHERE:

AN ONGOING LIST OF

THINGS I LIKE ABOUT MYSELF

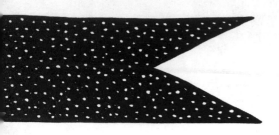

#selfie ♡

Catalog of good things

(A) Daydreams about my future self.

(B) This cute memory from my childhood.

(C) This scene from my favorite tv show or movie.

(D) My most-loved item of clothing.

(E) Reason to celebrate!

(A)

(B)

120

8AM

10AM

START HERE

my Perfect

MIDNIGHT

8PM

MIDDAY

2PM

6PM   4PM

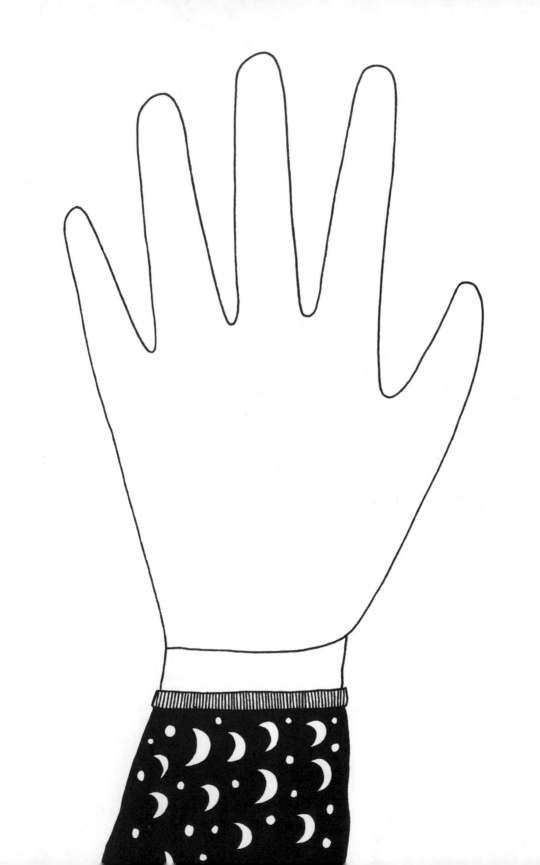

5 REASONS WHY I DESERVE A HIGH FIVE RIGHT NOW

1

2

3

4

5

IT'S A COLD & RAINY DAY!
WHAT FUN THINGS CAN YOU DO?

IT'S A WARM & SUNNY DAY!
WHAT FUN THINGS CAN YOU DO?

THE **PERKS** OF BEING .... YEARS OLD!
(current age)

① Finally I can ....
....
....

② This is the year ....
.... came into my life!

③ Wisdom I have now that I didn't have last year:

....
....
....

④ My ....
.... has never looked better!

⑤ Last year I could only wish for ....
....
.... and now it's actually happening!

129

NICE MOMENTS SPENT
inside MY COMFORT ZONE

FUN TIMES THAT HAPPENED outside MY COMFORT ZONE

A MEMORY THAT ALWAYS
MAKES ME SMILE

Advanced Diploma

- _____
- _____
- _____

Presented to

_____

Date:

MY HAPPY PLACE

WHEN YOU WERE A LITTLE HUMAN (SIX YEARS OLD!)
WHAT DID YOUR "HAPPY PLACE" LOOK LIKE?
DRAW EVERYTHING YOU CAN THINK OF!

ME

nice things people have said about me

✉ FROM:

💬 NEW COMMENT
FROM:

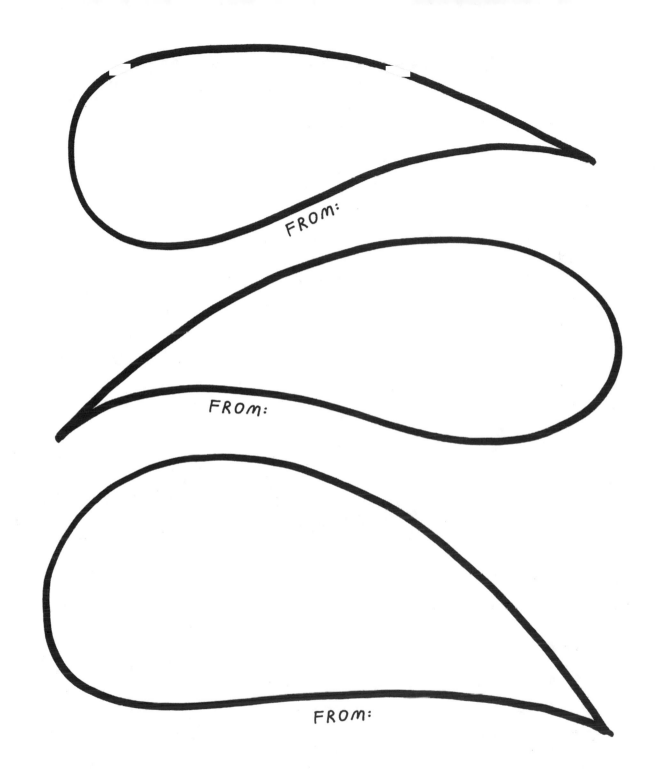

FROM:

FROM:

FROM:

* "PEOPLE" CAN BE FRIENDS, A TEACHER, SOMEONE
ON THE INTERNET, A STRANGER AT THE COFFEE SHOP.

MY GREATEST VICTORY

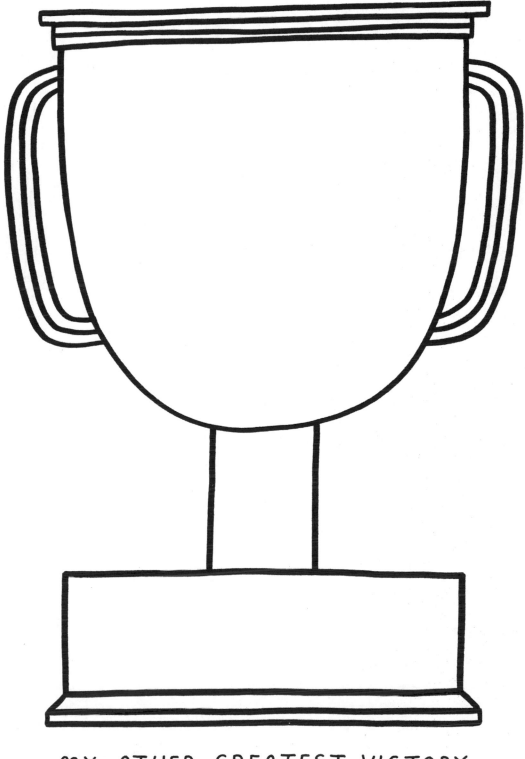

MY OTHER GREATEST VICTORY

YOUR NEW BUSINESS CARDS ARE HERE!
FILL IN YOUR NAME & DETAILS.

PRESIDENT

OF THE

FAN CLUB!

OFFICIAL TASTE TESTER

for

AT YOUR SERVICE!

Reigning Champion OF

(AND VERY HUMBLE HUMAN BEING)

MASTER OF MY OWN DESTINY!

SUCH A THOUGHTFUL GIFT!

☐ from _____   ☐ gift to self ♡

THE "me time" CLUB

YOUR NAME:

YOUR "ME TIME" SPECIALTY:

☐ DANCING AROUND THE HOUSE IN MY UNDERWEAR.

☐ EATING GUACAMOLE AND CORN CHIPS IN BED.

☐ TAKING A NAP.

☐

☐

☐

☐

HOW MANY MINUTES PER WEEK YOU WILL DEDICATE TO THE "ME TIME" CLUB:

✳ PLEASE NOTE MEMBERSHIP BEGINS WHEN YOU COMPLETE THIS FORM AND DRAW A SMILEY FACE IN THIS CIRCLE: ◯

WELCOME TO THE CLUB!

OUR BEST MEMORY TOGETHER:

the snack foods I love most

OUR BEST MEMORY TOGETHER:

PLOT TWIST!

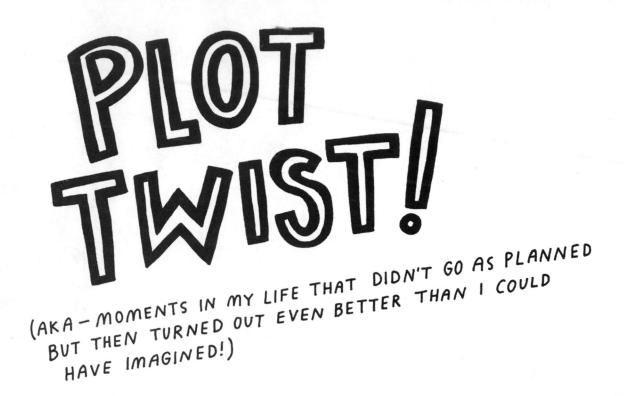

(AKA — MOMENTS IN MY LIFE THAT DIDN'T GO AS PLANNED
BUT THEN TURNED OUT EVEN BETTER THAN I COULD
HAVE IMAGINED!)

MY PLOT TWIST #1

MY PLOT TWIST #2

MY PLOT TWIST #3

design your own tattoos

AN INSIDE JOKE THAT MOST PEOPLE WON'T UNDERSTAND
A QUOTE THAT MEANS SOMETHING TO YOU
THE NAME OF YOUR "ONE TRUE LOVE"
A FACE YOU'LL NEVER GET TIRED OF LOOKING AT

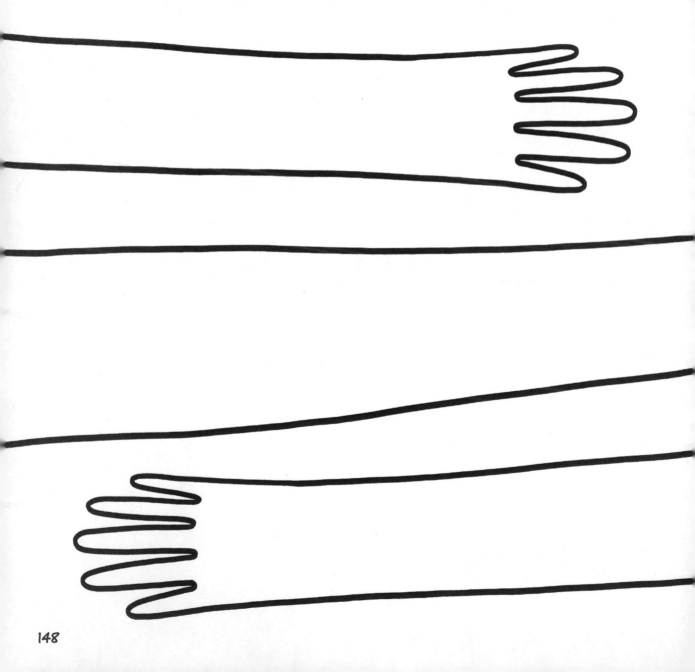

(YOUR NAME)

TATTOO PARLOUR

Now open for business!

the loves of

my life!

WELCOME HOME! ♡

HOME IS WHEREVER I'M WITH _____

_____

HOME IS WHERE THERE'S _____

ON THE KITCHEN BENCH AND _____

_____ IN THE FRIDGE.

HOME IS THE SMELL OF _____

AND _____

ANY PLACE CAN FEEL LIKE HOME IF I'VE

GOT MY _____

AND _____

AND OF COURSE _____

HOME IS KNOWING THAT _____

_____

HOME IS PERFECT WHEN _____
_____

AND I CAN _____

_____

MY FAVORITE "WELCOME HOME!" MOMENT
WAS WHEN _____

_____

_____

IF I COULD SUM UP WHAT HOME MEANS
TO ME IN ONE MEMORY IT'D BE _____

_____

_____

_____

_____

IF THE PLACE I CALL HOME HAD A NICKNAME
IT'D BE _____

thank you, stranger:

* write a letter to someone you've never met who's made your life better in some way.

DIARY of REALLY GOOD NAPS zᶻᶻ I'VE HAD

WHEN:

NAP LOCATION:

WHY THIS NAP WAS SO GOOD:

WHEN:

NAP LOCATION:

WHY THIS NAP WAS SO GOOD:

WHEN:

NAP LOCATION:

WHY THIS NAP WAS SO GOOD:

WHEN:

NAP LOCATION:

WHY THIS NAP WAS SO GOOD:

WHEN:

NAP LOCATION:

WHY THIS NAP WAS SO GOOD:

DESIGN *friendship bracelets* FOR YOUR MOST BELOVED *fictional characters* FROM BOOKS, MOVIES OR TV!

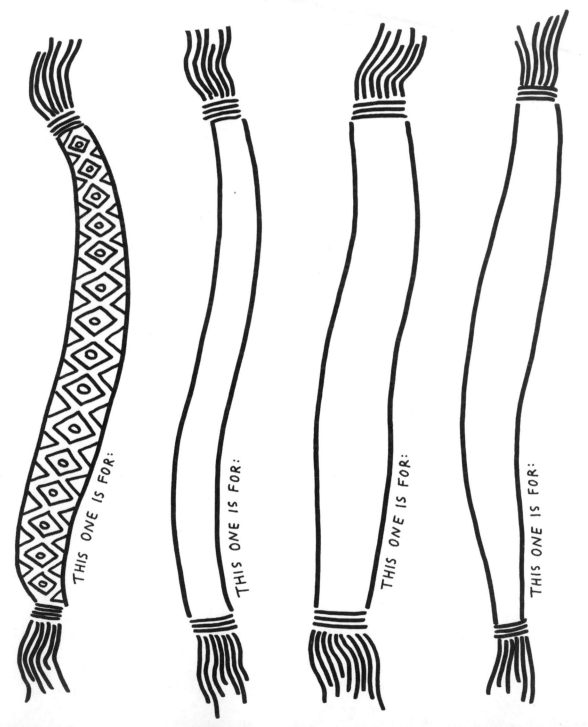

THIS ONE IS FOR:

THIS ONE IS FOR:

THIS ONE IS FOR:

THIS ONE IS FOR:

Ladies & Gentlemen!
The nominees for

BEST NICKNAME I'VE
EVER BEEN GIVEN

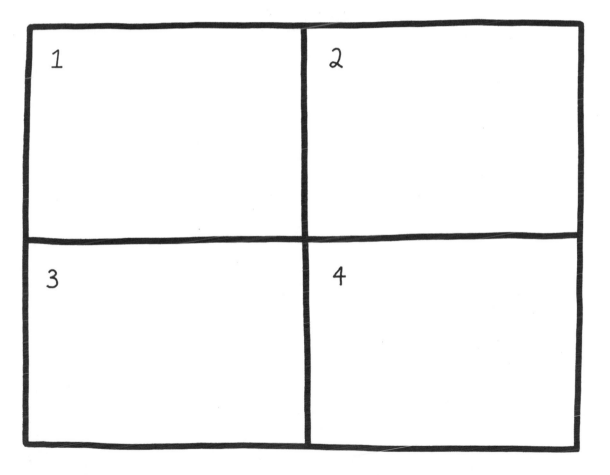

1	2
3	4

And the winner is...

THIS BATHROOM NEEDS A MAKEOVER.
DOODLE YOUR FAVORITE QUOTES ALL OVER
THE WALLS — GO NUTS!

Catalog of good things

(A) Something nice that arrived in the mail.

(B) My favorite type of flower.

(C) Taking the first delicious bite of...

(D) The sweetest dream I've had lately.

(E) my collection of...

(A)

(B)

REALLY WORKS!

A BEGINNER'S GUIDE: HOW

the fascinating life of

AN IN-DEPTH ANALYSIS OF LAST NIGHT'S EPISODE OF

THE TOPICS I COULD READ ABOUT (OR TALK ABOUT) FOR HOURS!

EVERYTHING THERE IS TO KNOW ABOUT

&

The   Aficionado

FROM:

FROM:

FROM:

167

HOW WE SPEND OUR days IS,
OF COURSE, HOW WE SPEND
OUR lives.

WHAT WE DO WITH this HOUR,
AND that ONE,
IS WHAT WE ARE DOING.

· annie dillard ·

23 GOOD WAYS to SPEND an HOUR

1.
2.
3.
4.
5.
6.
7.
8.
9.
10.
11.
12.
13.
14.
15.
16.
17.
18.
19.
20.
21.
22.
23.

(TRY TO THINK OF THINGS YOU DON'T NORMALLY DO
OR HAVE BEEN MEANING TO TRY)

IMPORTANT REMINDER:

ONE-PERSON KARAOKE PARTY THIS WEEK!

WHERE

☐ in the shower

☐ in the car

☐ in front of the bedroom mirror

☐

CHOICE OF FAKE MICROPHONE

☐ hairbrush ☐ tv remote ☐ banana

☐

YOUR IMAGINARY AUDIENCE

Who's sitting in the front row?

TOP SONG PICKS

THE SAPPY BALLAD

♫ _____

THE PARTY STARTER

♫ _____

THE ONE-HIT WONDER

♫ _____

THE GRAND FINALE

♫ _____

ENCORE!! ENCORE!!

♫ _____

the lyrics of a song that makes me want to

172

Cry in a good way because it's so Perfect

MY OWN PERSONAL BRAND OF
HAPPINESS©

TASTES LIKE:

LOOKS LIKE:

SMELLS LIKE:

SOUNDS LIKE:

FEELS LIKE:

GIFT BASKET TO CHEER ME UP

FOR CRUMMY DAYS & BAD MOODS!

what's inside...

* A HANDWRITTEN LETTER FROM _____

  TELLING ME _____

  _____

* DAILY SUPPLY OF _____

* THESE THREE MOVIES TO CHOOSE FROM:

  1 –

  2 –

  3 –

* GIFT CERTIFICATE FOR AN HOUR OF _____

  _____ WITH _____

* ALL THE INGREDIENTS TO MAKE _____

  _____

* AND OF COURSE:

5 REASONS TO BE EXCITED ABOUT THE FUTURE!

COMING SOON!

NEW!

BONUS! CUTE DRAWINGS for you TO CUT OUT AND PASTE THROUGHOUT THE BOOK!

DRAWN BY SOME OF MY FAVORITE ARTISTS ♡

JEM MAGBANUA! ALEXIS WINTER! MALLORY ROSE! BARBARA FONSECA!
JOSH LAFAYETTE! ALYSSA DUHE! GIADA GANASSIN! AIKAWA ERI!
RACHNA SOUN! JEFFREY D. PHILLIPS! CAITLIN CHILTON! DURU EKSIOGLU!
ADAM J. KURTZ! LAURA JAYNE HODKIN! INMA LORENTE! OKAT!

MUM, IT'S NOT AN EXAGGERATION TO SAY THIS BOOK WOULDN'T EXIST WITHOUT YOU. THANK YOU TO THE MOON AND BACK! ♡

THANK YOU, MARIAN (MY EDITOR) AND EVERYONE AT PERIGEE FOR BELIEVING IN ME AND BELIEVING IN THIS BOOK. I STILL HAVE TO PINCH MYSELF THAT YOU LET ME DO THIS!

THANK YOU, MEG — FOR EDITING MY FIRST TWO BOOKS WITH SUCH KINDNESS AND GUIDING ME INTO THIS DREAM JOB.

THANK YOU, SORCHE — FOR BEING MY AGENT AND ALLY IN NEW YORK.

TO MY FRIENDS AND FAMILY WHO MAKE ME LAUGH AND FEEL LOVED — THANK YOU! I LOVE YOU!

TO LENKA CLAYTON — I FIND ENDLESS JOY AND CURIOSITY IN YOUR IDEAS. THANK YOU FOR SHARING THEM.

TO KERI SMITH — YOU'RE THE REASON I EVER HOPED TO BECOME AN AUTHOR ONE DAY. THANK YOU FOR QUESTIONING WHAT A BOOK COULD BE.

AND TO YOU! HOLDING THIS BOOK! I OFTEN WONDER WHO YOU ARE AND WHAT YOU'LL DO WITH THESE PAGES. IT'S SO EXCITING TO THINK ABOUT.
THANK YOU FOR SUPPORTING THE THINGS I MAKE.
THANK YOU FOR INSPIRING ME TO MAKE MORE OF THEM!

love from — LISA x

PHOTO BY NICK DALE

LISA CURRIE IS THE AUTHOR OF me, you, us
AND the scribble diary. SHE CREATED THIS
BOOK FROM HER SUNNY BEDROOM IN MELBOURNE,
AUSTRALIA, WHERE SHE LIVES WITH FOUR FRIENDS
AND A DOG NAMED CHARLIE.

PRINTABLE SHEETS & OTHER PROJECTS:
WWW.LISACURRIE.COM

YOU CAN WRITE TO LISA HERE:
LISA CURRIE - PO BOX 200, CARLTON NORTH,
3054, VICTORIA, AUSTRALIA.

SHARE YOUR BOOK PAGES ♡
#THEPOSITIVITYKIT

OTHER BOOKS *by* LISA CURRIE

Available at all good bookstores!

me, you, us

A book to fill out together with your friends or a loved one. Write fortune cookies to each other! Decide on your perfect theme song! Brainstorm ideas for your matching tattoos!

SURPRISE yourself

Turn every day into a new beginning with this DIY happiness guide that will get you out of your head and into the world. Ready to try something new? Flip to any page and begin . . .

the scribble diary

Welcome to your own playful, personal doodling space—to vent your thoughts, reflect on your day, and jot down what's in your brain right now.